My Senses
SEEING

by
Grace Jones

Words written in **yellow** are explained in the glossary on page 24.

J612.84

CONTENTS

©This edition was published in 2018. First published in 2016.

Book Life
King's Lynn
Norfolk PE30 4LS

ISBN: 978-1-910512-69-2

All rights reserved
Printed in Malaysia

Written by:
Grace Jones
Designed by:
Drue Rintoul

A catalogue record for this book is available from the British Library.

WHAT ARE MY SENSES?

We all have five **senses**. They are sight, smell, taste, touch and hearing.

Your senses tell you what is going on around you.

HOW DO I SEE?

EYE

You use your eyes to see things around you.

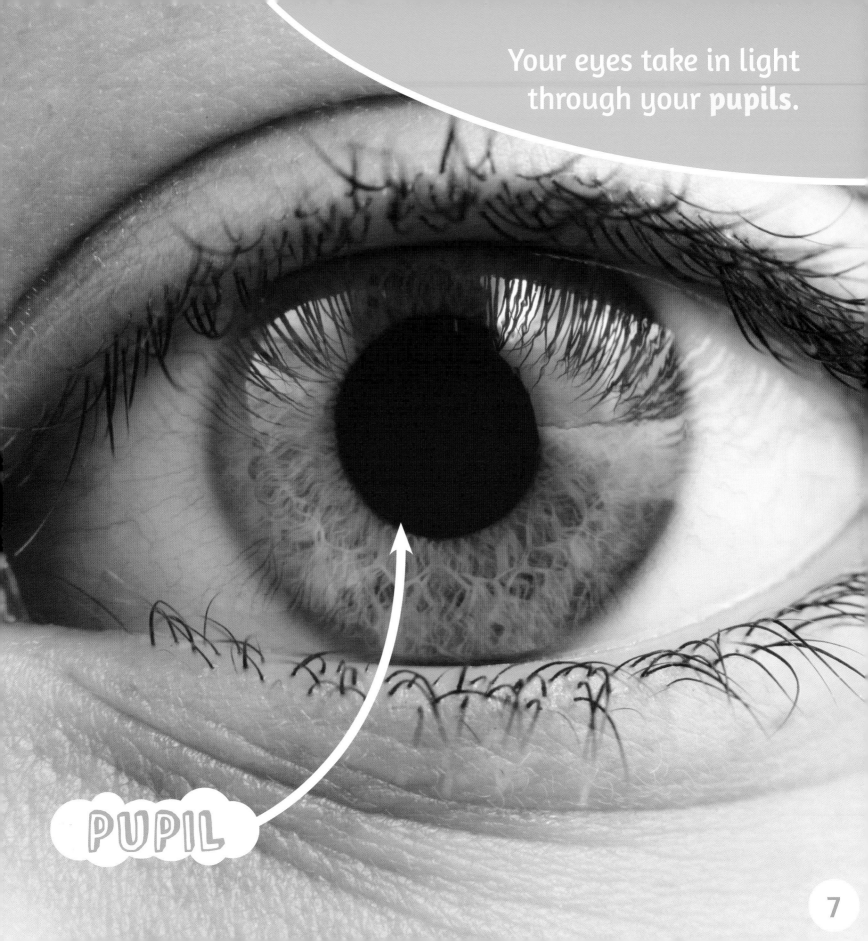

Your eyes take in light through your **pupils.**

PUPIL

YOUR LENS WORKS LIKE A CAMERA!

A special part of your eye, called the **lens**, makes a picture from the light.

The picture is sent to your brain. Your brain tells you what you are seeing.

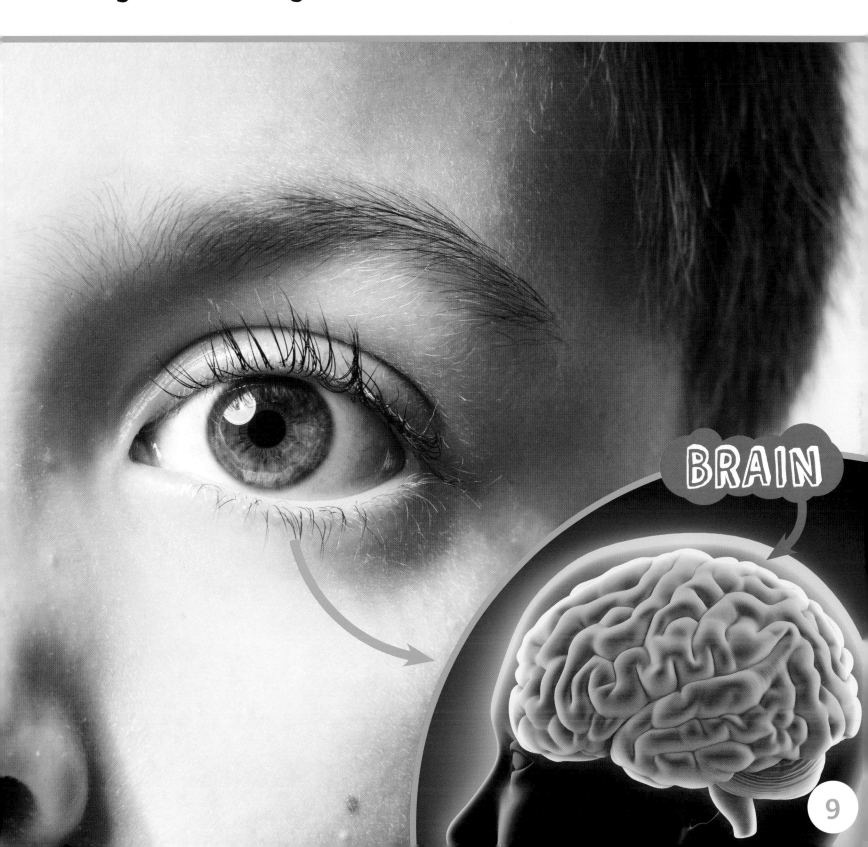

BRAIN

LIGHT AND DARK

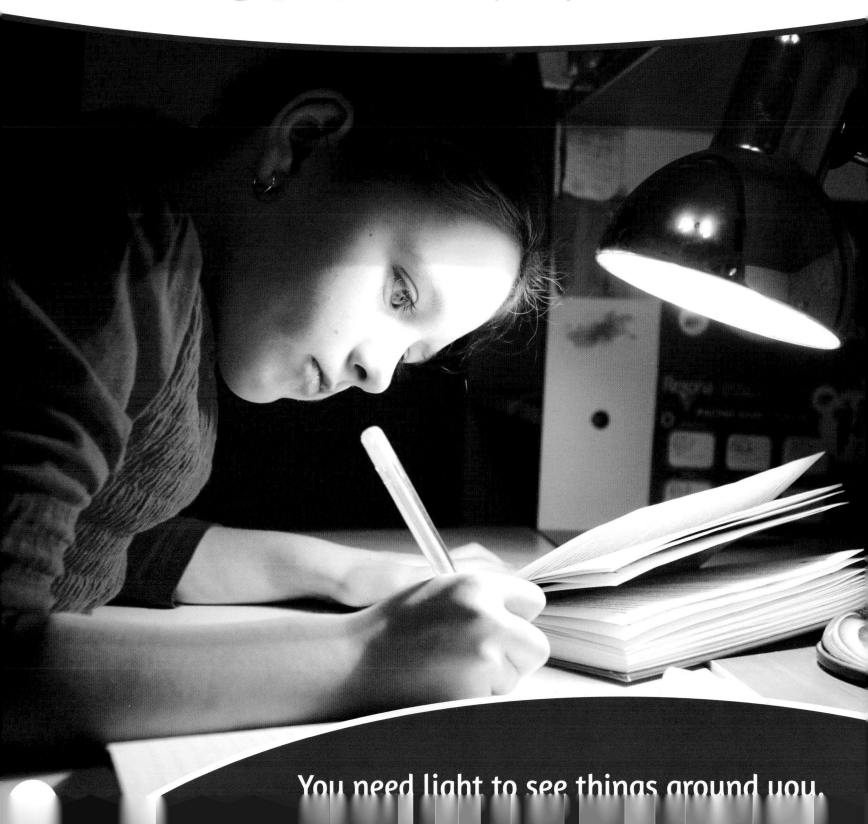

You need light to see things around you.

When it is dark, you cannot see.

DAY AND NIGHT

In the daytime, we use the light from the Sun to help us see.

At night, it is dark outside. We use other light to help us see.

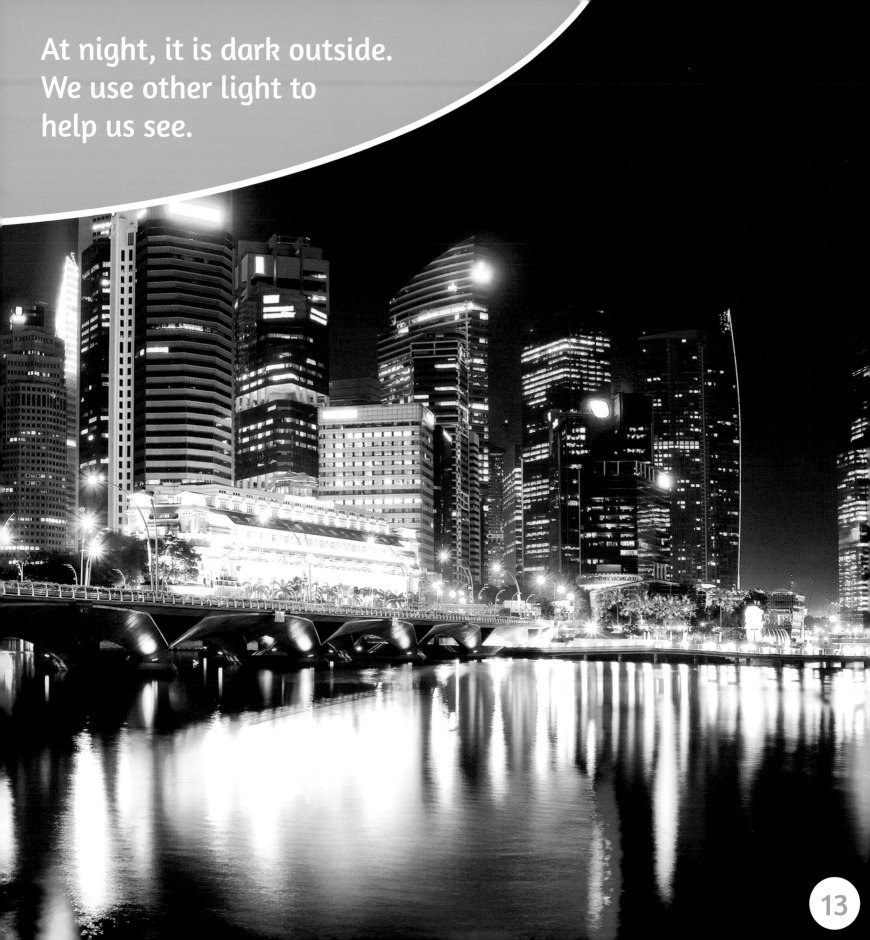

SEEING COLOUR

RAINBOW

Your eyes can see lots of different colours.

Seeing different colours can
help to keep you safe from danger.

STAYING SAFE

Your sense of sight helps you see warning signs.

When you see a red man at the traffic lights, you know it is unsafe to cross the road.

PEDESTRIANS
push button and wait
for signal opposite

WAIT

wait

cross
with care

AT THE SEASIDE

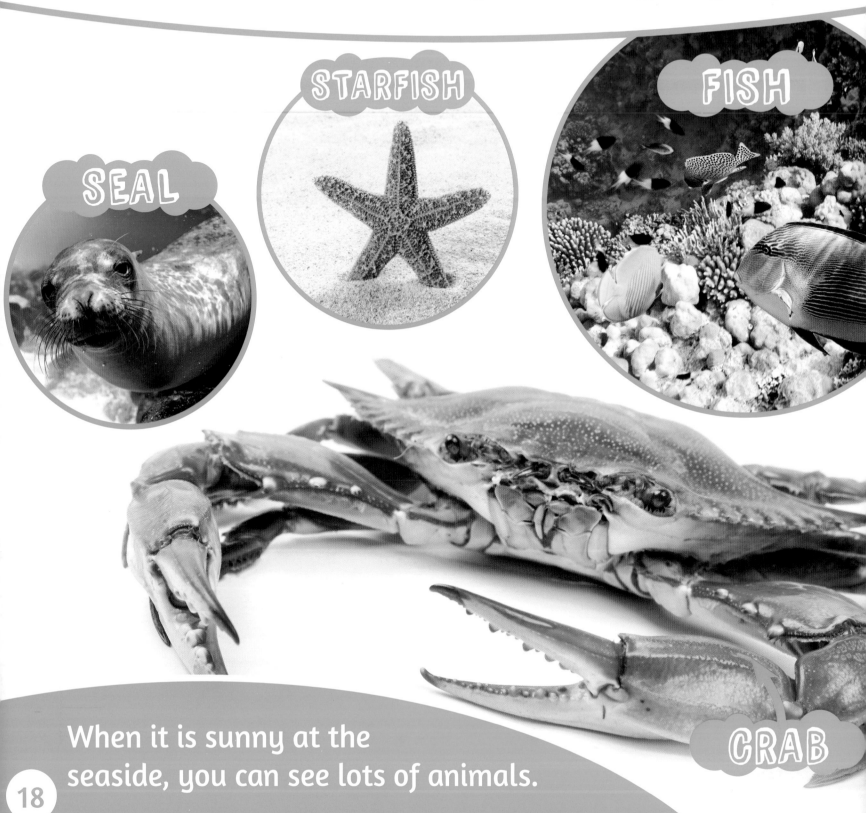

SEAL

STARFISH

FISH

CRAB

When it is sunny at the seaside, you can see lots of animals.

At night, the light from a lighthouse keeps boats safe.

LIGHTHOUSE

19

SUPER SENSES!

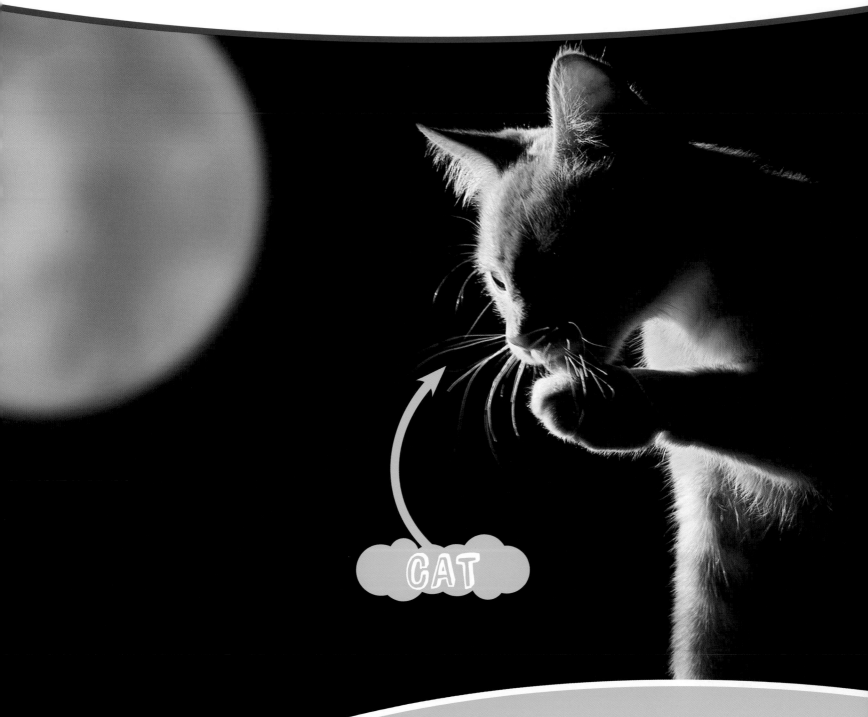

CAT

Some animals can see even when it is very dark.

This helps them to find food at night.

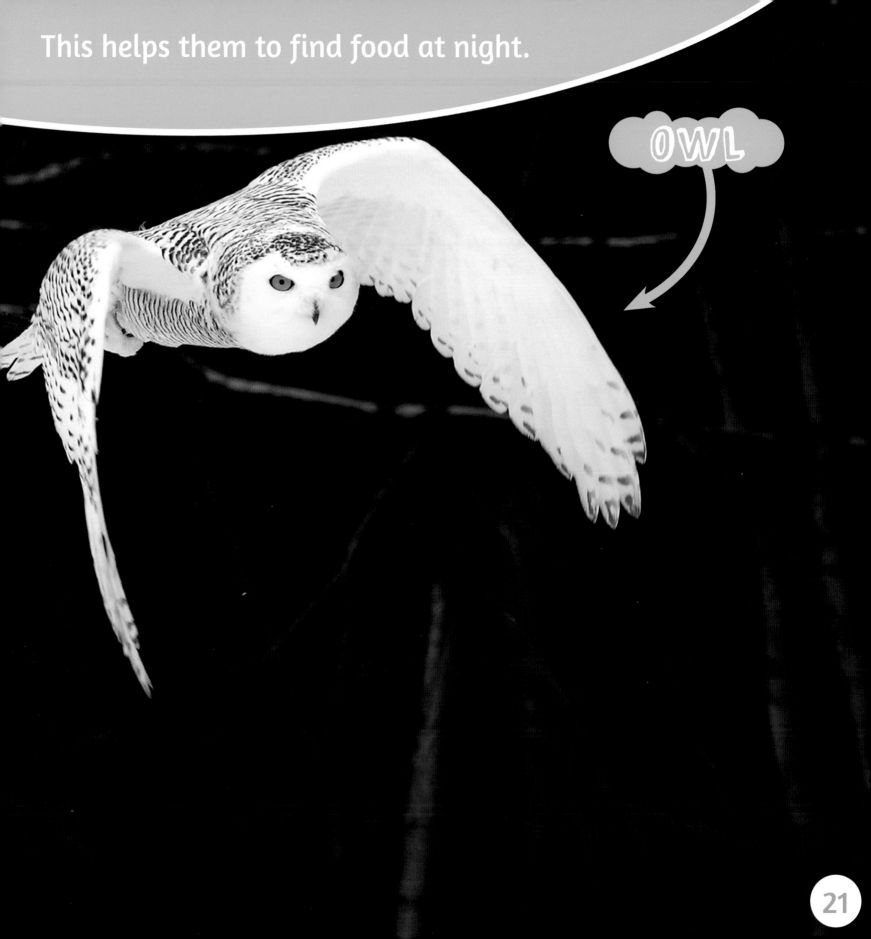

OWL

WHAT CAN YOU SEE?

Find a pencil and a piece of paper. Try to draw a picture of yourself with your eyes shut.

Now open your eyes. Draw another picture of yourself with your eyes open this time.

Look at the two pictures. Are they different? Which one was easier to draw? Why?

GLOSSARY

BRAIN
the organ in your head which tells your body what to do

LENS
part of your eye that makes a picture from light

PUPIL
part of your eye that takes in light

SENSES
the ways that your body tells you what is going on around you

WARNING SIGNS
signs that warn people of danger

INDEX